One Hundred and One Famous Poems

With a Prose Supplement

(Revised Edition)

An Anthology Compiled by
Roy J. Cook

THE REILLY & LEE CO.
PUBLISHERS -:- CHICAGO

LIBRARY OF CONGRESS
CATALOG CARD NO. 60-9006